Genre Expository Text

P9-BBT-046

Essential Question
What helps an animal survive?

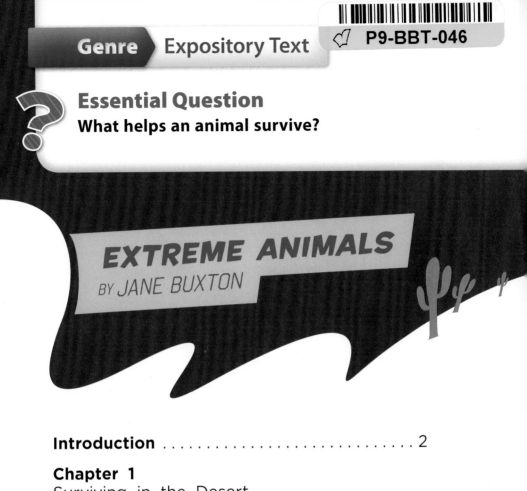

EXTREME ANIMALS
BY JANE BUXTON

INTRODUCTION

Planet Earth has many kinds of landscapes—from burning-hot deserts to frozen ice fields, and from oceans, rivers, and lakes to grassy plains, rain forests, and high mountains.

Animals can live in all of these **environments** because they have special **adaptations** to help them survive.

Many animals have adaptations that help them find food, live in different climates, and stay safe from **predators** that hunt them for food.

Some animal adaptations are physical adaptations. They may have thick fur to keep them warm or long legs to run away from predators. Others may have large ears to listen for **prey**, the animals they hunt for food. They also use their ears to hear a predator before it pounces.

Adaptations can be so extraordinary you wouldn't think of them in a million years!

The huge ears of the fennec fox help it to stay cool in the hot desert.

CHAPTER 1

SURVIVING IN THE DESERT AND THE RAIN FOREST

A desert is a harsh place for animals to live, and some have unusual ways of surviving. The Texas horned lizard has a strange way to keep itself safe. When a predator gets too close, the lizard squirts blood from its eyes. Then it puffs up its body so it looks too large for its enemy to swallow.

The horned lizard's sharp spines also protect it. A predator would have to be pretty hungry to try to eat one of these spine-covered lizards!

The Texas horned lizard blends into the desert background.

Javelinas keep safe by staying close to their family.

Another interesting desert animal is the javelina *(hah-ve-LEE-nah)*. This small, smelly, hairy animal looks like a pig.

To scare off a predator, such as a coyote, the javelina boldly faces the animal. It makes a clattering noise with its teeth. It raises the stiff hairs on its back to make itself look bigger, then it charges. The javelina also gives off a strong smell as a warning to the herd when it is startled. This smell is so strong that javelinas are also called "stink pigs."

If you're a javelina with a hairy, smelly family around you, there's a good chance you can make a predator change its mind!

You might think a rain forest would be easier to live in than a desert. After all, there's plenty of food and water in a rain forest. But that also means a lot of animals live there.

Being able to climb trees is a useful skill in the rain forest. It allows an animal to keep away from predators. The sloth spends most of its life in the treetops. Its strong, curved claws help it climb and hang upside down from branches.

The sloth also moves very slowly. It does this so it's not noticed. Green algae grows in its fur. This camouflages the sloth in the treetops.

Sloths hang upside down 24 hours a day.

The aye-aye has big, round eyes that allow it to see well at night.

The aye-aye lives only in the rain forests of Madagascar, near Africa. It hunts beetle larvae, which live inside rotting wood. The aye-aye gnaws a narrow hole in the wood with its sharp teeth. Then it hooks out the larvae with a long, skinny finger. The aye-aye is **nocturnal**. This helps it to stay safe from daytime predators.

However, the aye-aye is **endangered** and may soon become **extinct**. People have hunted it because they think it brings bad luck. Also, much of the rain forest in Madagascar has been cut down, destroying the aye-aye's habitat. Today there are laws to keep people from hunting it.

CHAPTER 2

WATERY ENVIRONMENTS

Most **mammals** are best suited for living on land, but some have special adaptations for living in water. The Florida manatee is a gentle mammal with a smooth body, a strong tail, and two front flippers. It has a layer of blubber, or fat, under its skin to keep it warm. These things help manatees live in the water.

A manatee's top lip has two parts that move separately, like fingers. This helps the manatee to grab onto a plant and put it into its mouth.

Jim Reid/USFWS

Manatees eat seagrass and other water plants.

Not all mammals are what they seem. The duck-billed platypus has webbed feet and a bill. It may seem like a duck, but it's actually a four-legged mammal!

Although it's a mammal, the platypus lays eggs. When the eggs hatch, the young platypuses drink milk from their mother.

The duck-billed platypus lives in Australia. It makes its home by digging tunnels in the banks of streams or rivers. It swims with its nostrils, ears, and eyes closed. When it feels the vibrations of small creatures, it uses its rubbery bill to catch them. To keep safe from predators, the male platypus has poisonous spikes on its legs.

A Trick Animal

When scientists first saw a duck-billed platypus in the late 1700s, they couldn't believe this strange creature was real. They were sure it was a trick. They thought someone had joined a duck's bill onto the body of a beaver-like animal.

Amphibians are animals that can live on land and in the water. They have lungs for breathing on land. They can also breathe through their skin in the water. Frogs, toads, and salamanders are all amphibians.

One of the strangest toads is the Surinam toad. It lives in South America in muddy ponds and swamps. After a female toad has laid her eggs, the eggs sink into the skin on her back.

After several weeks, the eggs hatch. The tiny toads grow. When they are two or three months old, the toads climb out of their mother's skin and swim away. This adaptation keeps the eggs and babies safe from predators.

Baby Surinam toads will hatch from the black spots on this mother's back.

Another weird amphibian is the Chinese giant salamander. The Chinese giant salamander is the largest amphibian in the world. It can grow to nearly 6 feet in length.

Although this salamander has lungs, it breathes mainly through its skin because it spends most of its life in the water. The giant salamander also has two flaps of skin that give it a bigger surface area for breathing.

The Chinese giant salamander has bad eyesight. To catch prey, it uses its sense of smell and its ability to feel movement in the water.

CHAPTER 3

WEIRD CREATURES OF THE DEEP

The deep ocean is the largest habitat on Earth. It's extremely dark in the deep ocean, and the water pressure is very strong. Creatures that live in this habitat have adaptations that allow them to survive these conditions.

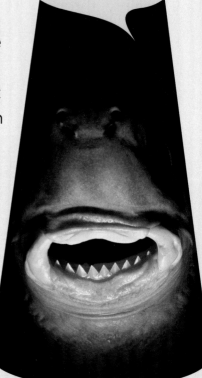

The cookie cutter shark has strong, sharp teeth.

The underside of a cookie cutter shark's body glows in the dark. When fish look up from below, they can't see the shark because it's camouflaged against the light from the ocean's surface.

On the shark's jaw, there's a small patch with no light. When a fish mistakes this small dark patch for a small fish and swims closer, the shark attacks. Its strong lips latch onto the fish, and its upper teeth sink into the fish's flesh. Then it digs its sharp "cookie cutter" teeth in and spins around. This cuts out a neat circle of flesh to eat.

The blobfish is an odd-looking fish that lives in deep water near Australia. Few other fish can cope with the water pressure at this depth.

However, the blobfish has no muscle. It has jelly-like flesh that is lighter than water. This allows the blobfish to float because the pressure inside its body is similar to the pressure of the water. Since it has no muscle, it can't move itself around to hunt for prey. Instead, it floats, waiting for food to drift close to it.

Accidental Catch

The blobfish has a fold of skin on it that looks like a nose. From the front, it looks strangely like a human face.

People don't eat blobfish. However, when huge nets are dropped into the ocean to catch crabs, lobsters, and other seafood, they unfortunately catch blobfish by accident. This could cause the blobfish to become extinct.

There are many different habitats and many interesting ways that animals survive. But will all of these animals continue to survive?

To help it survive, an animal needs a healthy habitat. Many habitats are destroyed when people pollute the water or cut down trees to build towns. People also hunt animals. This has caused many animals to become endangered or extinct.

Conservationists and scientists work hard to protect wild animals and their environments. We can all help to protect our planet and its amazing animals.

Animals like the jaguar are endangered.

Alan and Sandy Carey/Photodisc/Getty Images

Summarize

Use details from *Extreme Animals* to summarize how animals have adapted to survive. Your graphic organizer may help you.

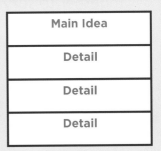

| Main Idea |
| Detail |
| Detail |
| Detail |

Text Evidence

1. How do you know that *Extreme Animals* is an expository text? GENRE

2. What is the main idea of the first paragraph on page 4? Use key details to support your response. MAIN IDEA AND KEY DETAILS

3. What is the meaning of the word *unfortunately* on page 13? Use what you know about prefixes to help you figure it out. PREFIXES

4. Write about how creatures in the deep ocean survive. Include details from the text in your answer. WRITE ABOUT READING

Compare Texts

Read about how some animals worked together to survive.

HARE AND THE WATER

The fierce African sun had dried the grass to a pale, yellowish brown. Beneath the grass, thousands of cracks split the ground.

Hare hopped across the dry landscape. "Giraffe," he said, "where's the nearest waterhole?"

"Don't you know there's a drought?" said Giraffe.

"Yes," said Hare, "but there must be water somewhere."

"Let's look together," said Giraffe. "I'm pretty thirsty."

"Sure!" replied Hare. "Follow me!"

Soon they met an extremely bony animal. "Water," said Antelope weakly.

"You need water? Follow me!" said Hare.

Soon the three animals came across Lion and Elephant, who were looking for water together.

"Just follow me," said Hare importantly.

Illustration: Bob Brugger

16

"Excuse me!" grumbled Tortoise. Threading her way through the animals' legs, she plodded to the front of the group.

Tortoise announced, "There's an old, dry waterhole ahead. If we go there together, we can all dig for water."

At the dry waterhole, Lion spoke. "We all need water. Let's work together to find some."

All of the animals began digging. But after a few minutes, Hare flopped down in the shade. By the time the others noticed, Hare was fast asleep.

"That lazy hare!" fumed Lion.

"Look how he twitches in his sleep," muttered Tortoise. "He's probably dreaming about water."

"Let's watch him work while we take a rest," said Antelope.

The others woke Hare and made him dig.

At first Hare flexed his muscles, showing off as he dug, but he soon grew tired and slowed down.

"We'll never find water at this rate. Come on, team!" Tortoise said.

The animals all started digging again. Soon, they struck water. It was muddy, but nobody complained. Water dribbled down Hare's chin as he drank.

"Working together works," said Hare.

"Congratulations, Hare!" said Tortoise. "You finally figured it out!"

Make Connections

How do the animals find water?
ESSENTIAL QUESTION

What are some of the things animals need to survive? Use examples from *Extreme Animals* and *Hare and the Water* in your answer. **TEXT TO TEXT**

Glossary

adaptations *(a-dap-TAY-shuhnz)* special traits that help living things survive *(page 2)*

amphibians *(am-FI-bee-uhnz)* animals that can live on land and in water *(page 10)*

endangered *(en-DAYN-jurd)* at risk of dying out *(page 7)*

environments *(en-VIGH-ruhn-muhnts)* the surroundings where animals live *(page 2)*

extinct *(eks-TINKT)* describes a species that has died out *(page 7)*

mammal *(MA-muhl)* a warm-blooded animal that feeds its young with milk *(page 8)*

nocturnal *(nok-TUR-nuhl)* active at night *(page 7)*

predators *(PRE-duh-turz)* animals that hunt other animals for food *(page 2)*

prey *(pray)* animals that are hunted for food *(page 3)*

Index

Focus
on
Science

Purpose To show how adaptations help an animal survive

Procedure

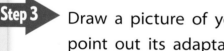

Step 1 Work with a partner to invent a new animal. Select a habitat for your animal to live in. It can be a desert, rain forest, or sea creature.

Step 2 Decide what adaptations your animal has developed. How does it stay safe from predators, find food, and cope with the climate in its environment?

Step 3 Draw a picture of your animal. Add labels that point out its adaptations.

Step 4 Give your animal a name. Present your animal to the class, explaining where it lives and why it needs each adaptation.

Conclusion What have you learned about the ways different animals survive in the places they live? Different environments have different dangers, and each animal has had to find ways to survive.